Green Bean's

Got Talent

By: Brenda Anderson

Https://brendaskidsbooks.com

Printed and produced in
United States of America

978-1-7352850-1-6 Softcover
978-1-7352850-0-9 Hardcover

Dedicated to you:

May you discover and develop your talents while bringing joy to others.
May you cheer others on and encourage them to do their
best...

A special thanks to all who help and encourage me.
I love and appreciate you all!

"Good morning, Grandma," Holland said cheerfully as he bounced into the kitchen. "What are we eating for breakfast? I am starved!"

With the sound of Holland's voice, the baby kestrel falcons began squawking in the laundry room. "I think Red, Yellow, Blue, and Green Bean are ready for breakfast," laughed Holland.

"I guess your breakfast will have to wait," Grandma commented with a smile.

"We better get that noisy bunch of chicks fed first."

"I think their squawks are louder than my growling stomach!" Holland replied.

Grandma took the baby kestrel falcons' food from the refrigerator and began cutting it into small pieces.
Grandpa and Eliza joined Grandma and Holland in the kitchen.

"I think the babies get noisier every day! We can add that to the list of talents they are practicing," grinned Grandpa. "Did you know it has been three weeks since we rescued them from the tree after the big storm?"

"I can't believe how big they have grown," said Eliza as she walked into the laundry room. Eliza reached inside the incubator and gently picked up Green Bean.

"I think it is time for us to build them a new home. They need some place to perch in the incubator," stated Grandpa.

"That would be fun! Can I help you Grandpa?" Holland asked.

"Sure," grinned Grandpa. "But first Holland, can you help me feed these hungry little birds while Grandma fixes breakfast? We can go to the shop after we eat and build the little birds a new perch to sit on."

Holland loved to help Grandpa in his shop. "I always learn so much when I help you, Grandpa." said Holland.

Holland gobbled his breakfast quickly. He didn't want to take a chance of missing out on the project.

"Grandma,
can I
help
you?"
Eliza
asked.
"Maybe we can
make cookies to
take to Grandpa
and Holland
for a snack."

"Hey, what about me?" grinned Uncle Spencer, as he walked into the kitchen. "Will you share those cookies with me too?"

"Uncle Spencer, I am so happy you are here!" cheered Holland. "Can you help me and Grandpa make a new perch for the baby kestrel falcons? They need more room to practice their talents."

"I think that is a good idea!" Grandpa is so talented when it comes to building projects," replied Uncle Spencer, as they went to the shop to work on their project.

Grandma and Eliza cleaned up the breakfast dishes and began making cookies. Eliza loved to help Grandma in the kitchen.

Eliza loved Grandma to tell stories of when she was a little girl and stories about her family. The sweet smell of cookies filled the air as they chatted.

Can it be dinner time already?" exclaimed Grandma, just as the back door swung open.

"Yes, it is!" said Grandpa as he stepped through the door, followed by Holland and Uncle Spencer. "And we are starving!" said Holland.

Grandma grinned as she commented. "You are always starving Holland. I don't think we can ever fill you up!"

Holland laughed at Grandma's remark. "I don't think I am the only one always hungry! Just listen to those noisy baby birds in the laundry room!"

Once again, Grandma took the food from the refrigerator and started to cut the meat into tiny pieces to feed the baby falcons.

Impatiently waiting in the laundry room on the counter were Red, Yellow, Blue, and Green Bean.

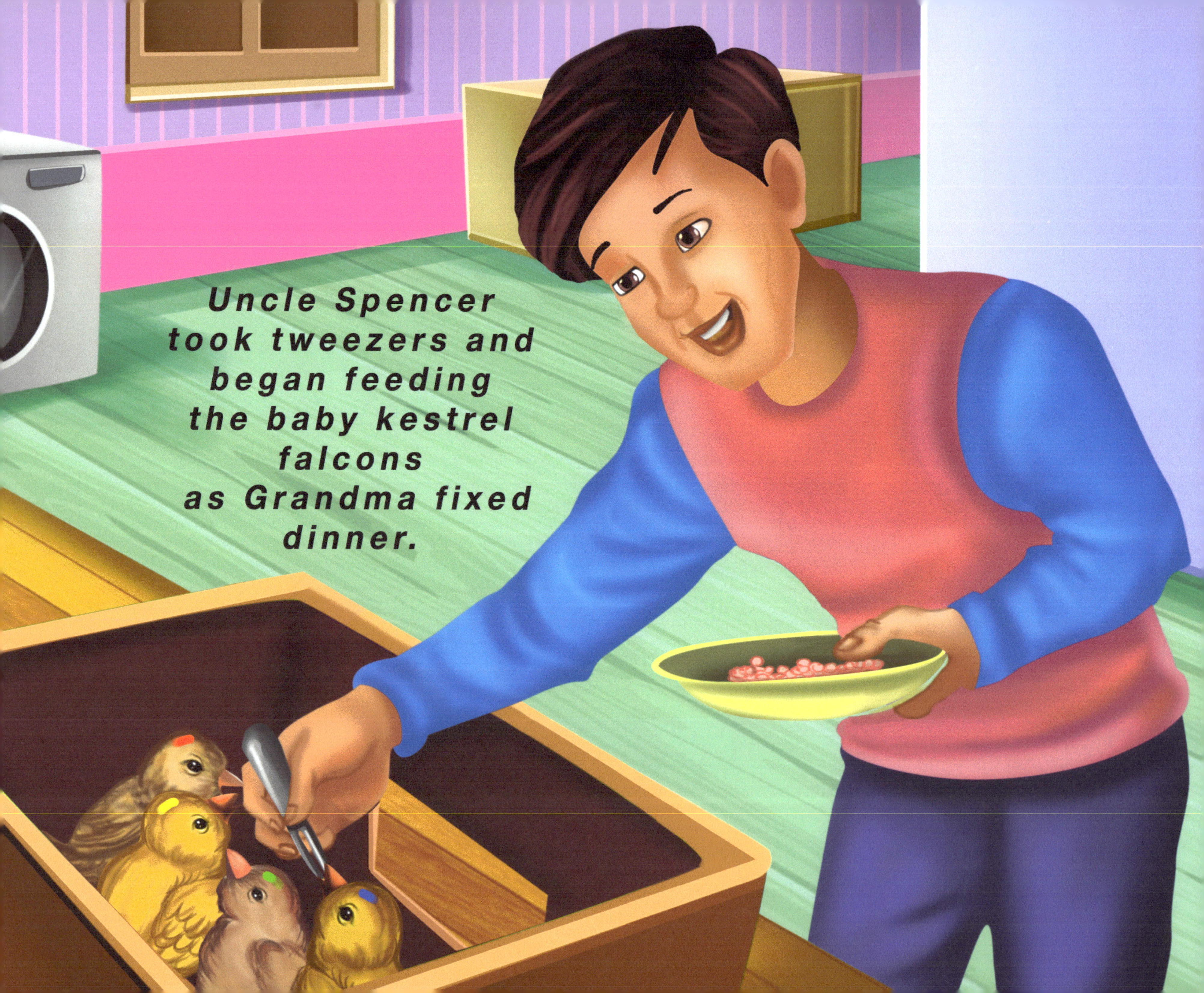

Uncle Spencer
took tweezers and
began feeding
the baby kestrel
falcons
as Grandma fixed
dinner.

"Thank you for dinner. It is really good!" exclaimed Grandpa as they sat around the dinner table discussing the day's events.

"Grandma is a really good cook. That is why I eat so much!" smiled Holland.

"We finished our project," Grandpa stated.

"After dinner we will move the baby falcons onto their new perch. They are going to like having the extra room to practice their talents!"

Red, Yellow, Blue and Green Bean squawked with excitement as Grandpa set up their new perch. "With all these places to sit, it will make a good home for them. They will have room to move around. With all the different perches, they can practice hopping from place to place and use their wings to learn to fly." said Grandpa.

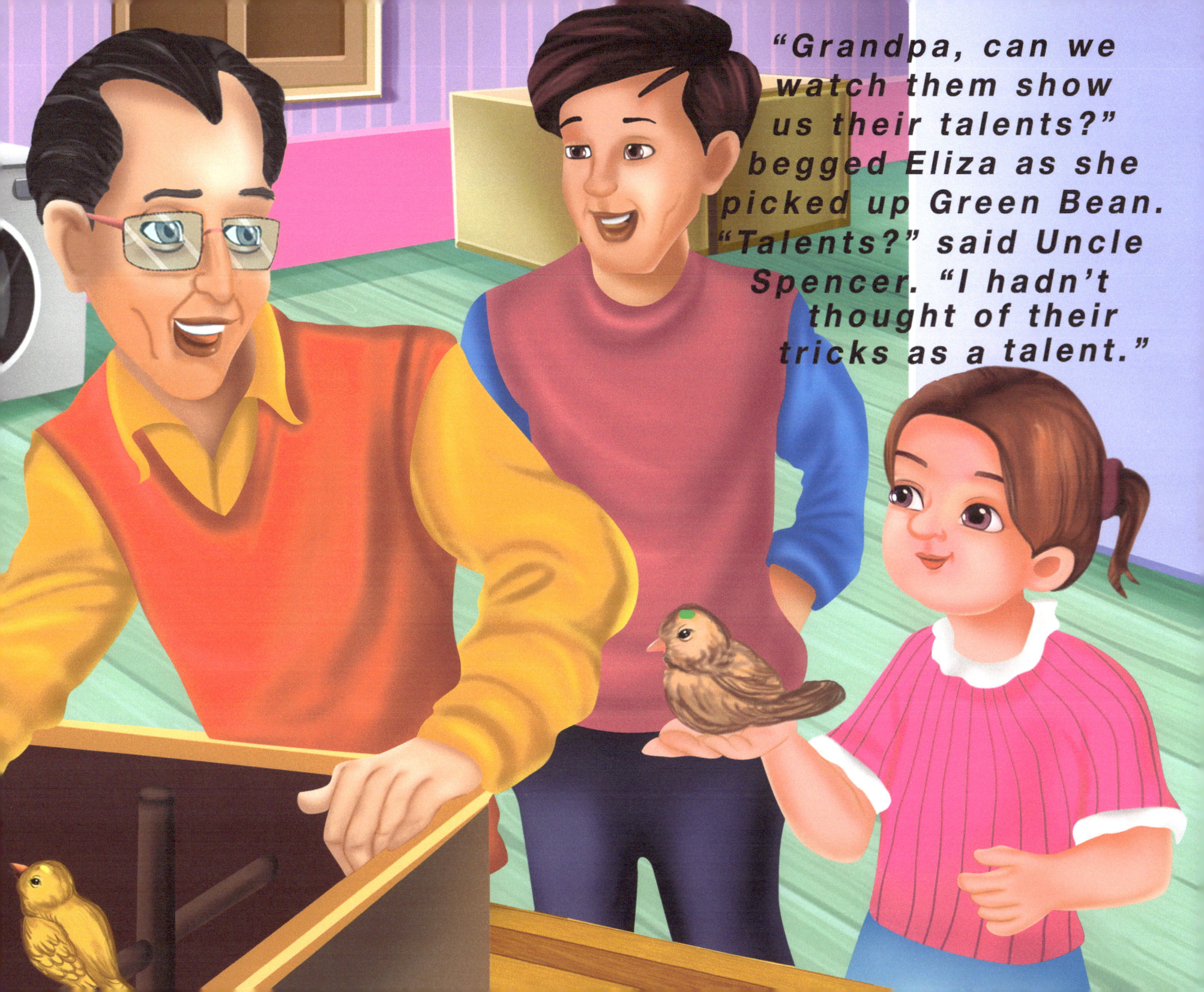

"Grandpa, can we watch them show us their talents?" begged Eliza as she picked up Green Bean. "Talents?" said Uncle Spencer. "I hadn't thought of their tricks as a talent."

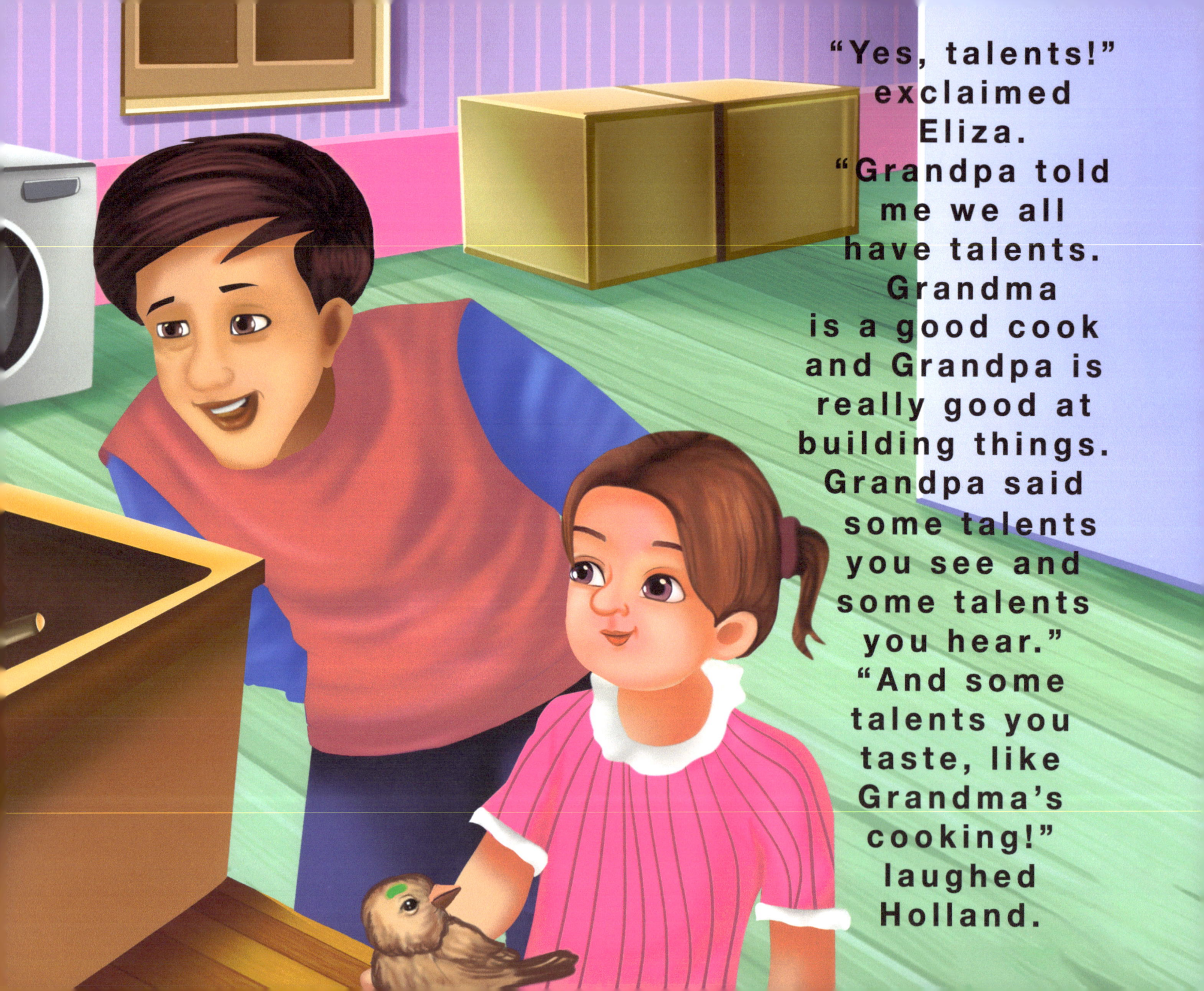

"Yes, talents!" exclaimed Eliza. "Grandpa told me we all have talents. Grandma is a good cook and Grandpa is really good at building things. Grandpa said some talents you see and some talents you hear."

"And some talents you taste, like Grandma's cooking!" laughed Holland.

Grandma laughed, "When we share our talents, it can bring joy to others, even cooking. Let's see if Red is ready to share her talent." Grandma lifted Red out of the incubator, setting the bird gently on her arm. "Sing Red," Grandma said with a smile.

Red stood tall and stretched out her little neck. A beautiful song carried through the air. Everyone listened as Red chirped and sang, sharing her beautiful music. When Red finished, she settled back on Grandma's hand.

Green Bean began to screech and flap his wings, cheering for Red. Everyone cheered and clapped.

"That was
beautiful!"
whispered Eliza,
as she stroked
Red gently on
the neck.
"What a wonderful
talent you have,
Red!"

"Yellow, it is your turn to share your talent. Yellow is a great dancer!" stated Grandpa as he lifted Yellow from the Perch and set him carefully on the counter.

Yellow was so excited to perform. He began
to shuffle across the counter, sharing his
fancy dance moves.

Green
Bean began to
to screech and flap his
wings, cheering for Yellow.
Everyone cheered for Yellow as
he finished performing.

Yellow hopped onto Grandpa's hand and then onto his new perch.

"That is a fun talent!" giggled Eliza.

Blue was so excited for his turn to perform. He quickly jumped off the perch onto Grandpa's arm. Blue took another giant leap onto the counter.

"Blue is a great jumper!" grinned Grandpa.

Blue jumped up and down, shuffled around, and then jumped some more. He loved the cheers and laughter coming from the audience, but most of all he loved the way Green Bean was flapping his wings and cheering for him.

Blue jumped onto Grandpa's arm and then jumped onto his new perch. "Blue is a great jumper!" cheered Holland. "I think the kestrel falcons are so much fun to watch!"

Eliza grinned, as she snuggled up close to Green Bean.

"Grandpa, what is Green Bean's talent?" Eliza asked.

Grandpa looked at Eliza
thoughtfully.
"What do you think Green
Beans talent is?"
he asked.

Eliza and Holland looked at each other with a puzzled look on their faces. "Grandpa, you told us how some talents are hidden and we don't notice them. Does Green Bean have a hidden talent?" asked Holland.

"Good, Holland!" said Grandpa. "Do you remember when the other chicks were performing? Green Bean was cheering and flapping his wings. He was cheering for his friends, showing them love."

"Green Bean's talent is to be a good friend!" exclaimed Eliza. "Cheering for others makes Green Bean happy!" added Grandma.

"We all have great talents," laughed Uncle Spencer. "Watch my talent!" He reached over and carefully took Green and Red from Eliza and Grandma. He gently placed them on his arm. Stepping over to the perch, Yellow and Blue hopped onto his other arm.

Uncle Spencer
stretched out his
long arms and
grinned.

"What am I?

A telephone
pole!"
Uncle Spencer
laughed.

Everyone laughed
with Uncle Spencer
and his funny
sense of humor.

Green Bean was so excited. With
all the laughter he jumped on top of
Uncle Spencer's head. Green Bean
flapped his wings and screeched
with excitement.

Everyone laughed and cheered for Green Bean.

"Green Bean knows how to make you smile!" grinned Holland.

But the most important thing about Green Bean is....

being a good friend and helping others smile. This makes him happy, too!

The End

A kestrel falcon is also known as a sparrow hawk. They have interesting personalities. As you read in the story Red liked to sing. Grandpa would say, "sing red and she would sing," then he would say "thats enough" and she would stop. Yellow liked to jump around and blue would move around and looked as though he was dancing.

The Green Bean Series is based on a true story. A special thanks to this family for sharing their fun adventure and pictures while raising these little birds.

There are many things to learn about a kestrel. In order to have a bird of prey a license is required. Two people in this family have gone through training to learn to care for birds of prey. They are called licensed handlers. They have learned how to feed and care for these birds.

What will these little birds do next? Watch for the next Green Bean book to find out.

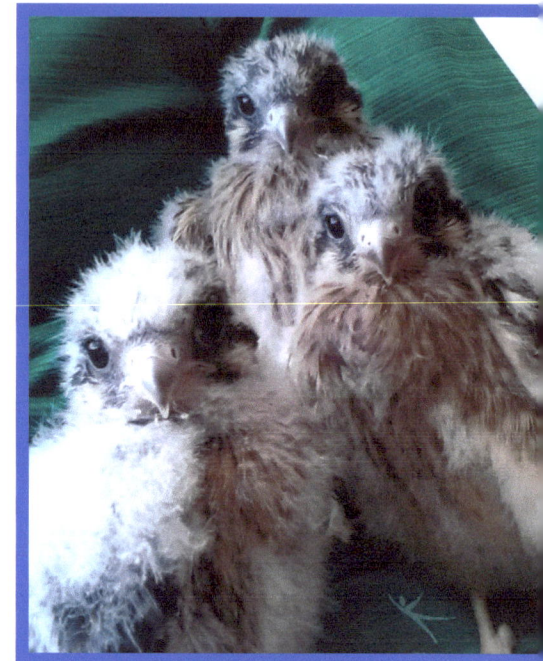

Brenda Anderson can usually be found with her husband Shawn on their farm in Idaho. Some of her favorite moments in life are spent with her family. She loves and enjoys spending time with her children and grandchildren.

Brenda has way too many hobbies including writing, blogging, gardening, and raising animals on their farm. Her love for animals is what inspired her to write children's books. She encourages all children to read. Reading opens doors to adventures for your imagination.

"Learn to love to read... Every book is a new adventure."

Green Bean Series

Book 1

**The Rescue of Green Bean is just the beginning.....
What Bean gains in this adventure is his greatest treasure.**

Based on a true story.

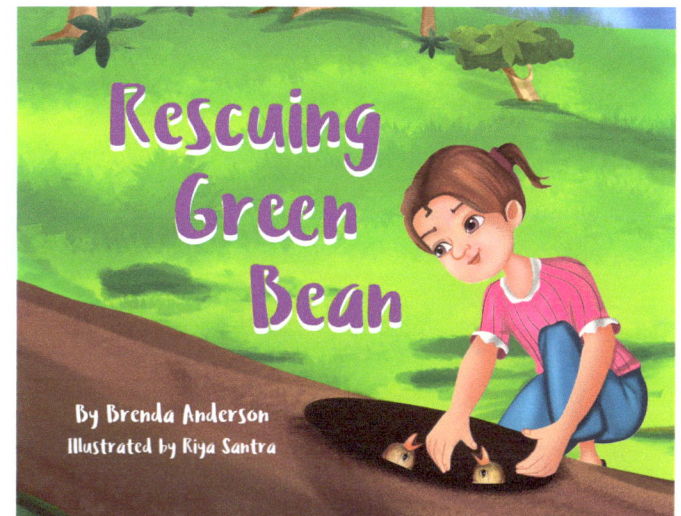

Rescuing Green Bean

By Brenda Anderson
Illustrated by Riya Santra

More books written by Brenda Anderson

The Farmers Wife Series

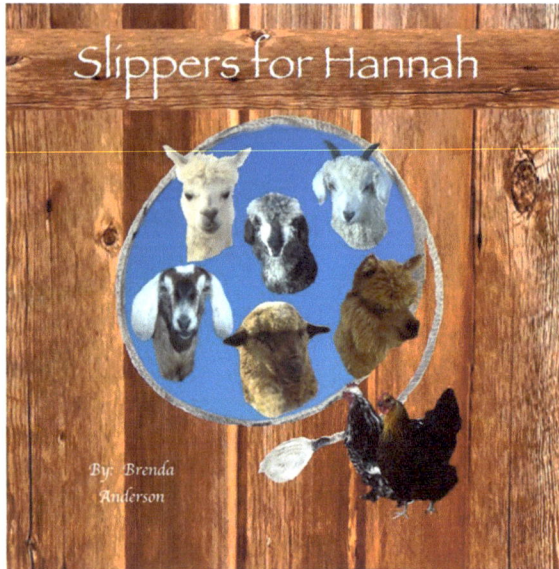

Slippers for Hannah
By: Brenda Anderson

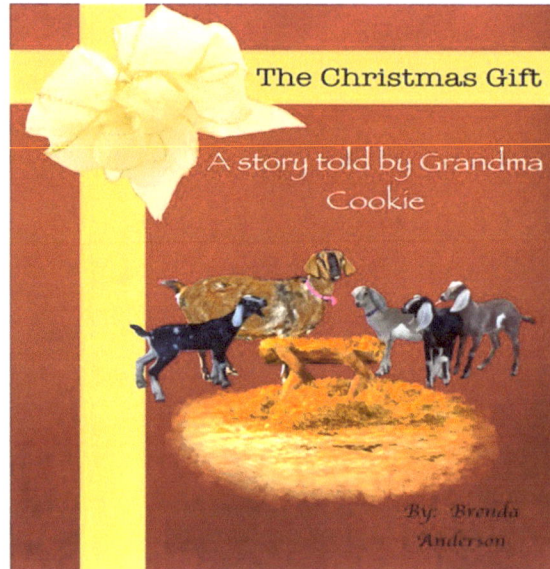

The Christmas Gift
A story told by Grandma Cookie
By: Brenda Anderson

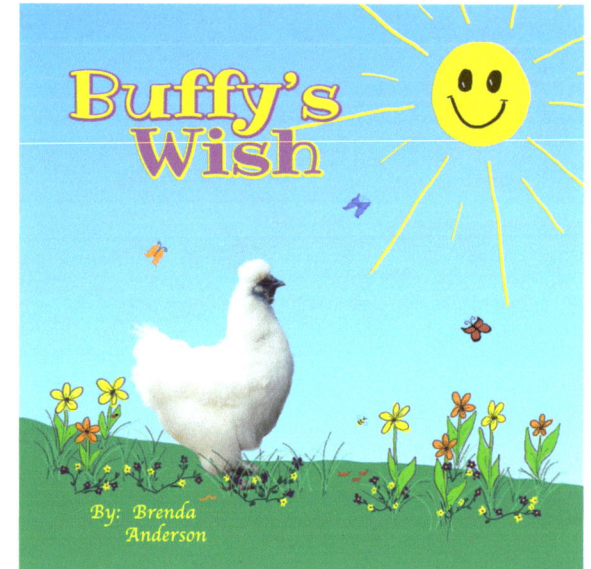

Buffy's Wish
By: Brenda Anderson

Puzzle Book

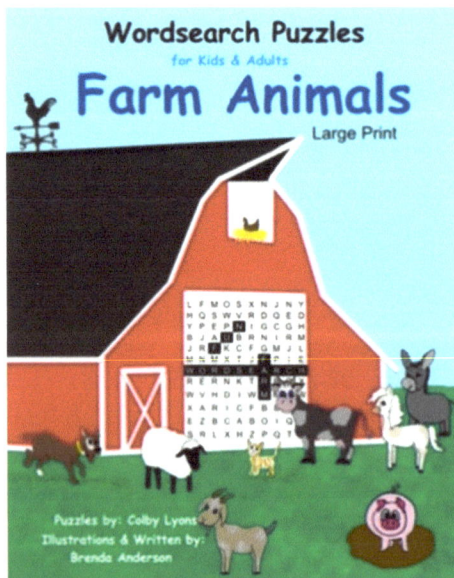

Wordsearch Puzzles
for Kids & Adults
Farm Animals
Large Print
Puzzles by: Colby Lyons
Illustrations & Written by: Brenda Anderson

You can find these books and more at:

Https://brendaskidsbooks.com

www.ingramcontent.com/pod-product-compliance
Lightning Source LLC
Chambersburg PA
CBHW041552030426

42336CB00004B/53